# The Baseball Brothers

By
Anne Fredrickson

Illustrated by
Kathryn Weaver

*To Duane, Emilia, Eric, Ellie and Kathryn*
*And all the Fredricksons who love baseball.*
*A.K.F.*


*To Mom and Dad, who always encouraged me.*
*K.M.W.*

ISBN: 978-0-615-20146-7
Library of Congress Control Number: 2008926186

# The Baseball Brothers

This is a story about my grandpa. His name was Herman.

Grandpa Herman had a lot of brothers. Their names were Fred, Martin, Axel, William, Nels, Joe, Edwin, Otto, Soren, Walter and Art. He also had four sisters named Hattie, Minnie, Elizabeth and Rose.

The boys and their sisters lived on a farm. They worked very hard. They milked cows in the morning, baled hay in the afternoon and cleaned the barn in the evening.

And for fun, Grandpa Herman and Fred, Martin, Axel, William, Nels, Joe, Edwin, Otto, Soren, Walter and Art played baseball. They loved baseball.

They played baseball after their chores were done. They played baseball in the shadows of the evening. They played baseball in the rain. They even played baseball in the snow.

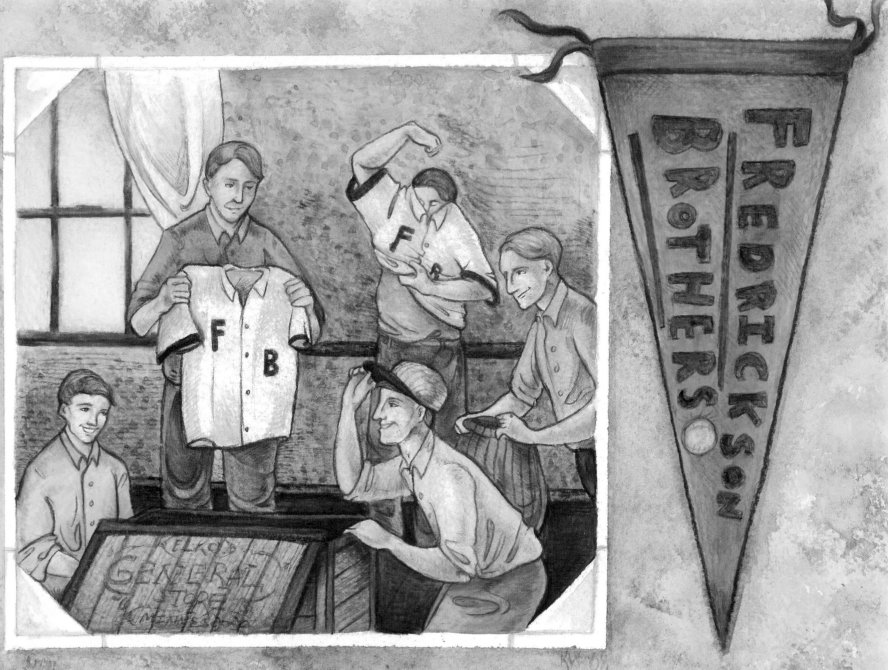

A long time ago, when my grandpa was a young man, his brother Otto asked the other brothers to join together to form a real baseball team. So Grandpa Herman and Fred, Martin, Axel, William, Nels, Joe, Edwin, Otto, Soren, Walter and Art became the Fredrickson Brothers Baseball Team.

There were enough brothers to have a player for every position on the team, plus a batboy and two coaches. Grandpa Herman played second base and center field.

For three years, Grandpa Herman and Fred, Martin, Axel, William, Nels, Joe, Edwin, Otto, Soren, Walter and Art traveled the countryside playing baseball every Sunday from the first crocus of spring until the first snowflakes of winter.

They were famous because people had never seen twelve brothers on one team before. Spectators came on horseback, riding in buggies and driving old black Model Ts. Fans came from all over to watch them play, partly because they were good and partly because they were exciting.

One time, Martin tackled a player for the other team as he ran toward home plate to score the winning run. Tackling is against the rules in baseball. The runner was very surprised. And his teammates were very upset. But they didn't want to get into an argument with Grandpa Herman and Fred, Martin, Axel, William, Nels, Joe, Edwin, Otto, Soren, Walter and Art!

In another game, Grandpa Herman scored an unassisted triple play. There were two runners on base when the batter hit toward center field. Grandpa Herman ran in toward second base and caught the fly ball for the first out. He turned a somersault, tagged second base for the second out, and chased down a runner for the third out. The inning was over with one swing of the bat!

When the brothers were batting, they were just as exciting. Otto, the catcher, was the best all-around player, and Grandpa Herman could hit into the outfield all day long. But when the game was on the line, Edwin was the brother to have at the plate. He never struck out once in three years!

Grandpa Herman and Fred, Martin, Axel, William, Nels, Joe, Edwin, Otto, Soren, Walter and Art played their best baseball at the county fair in 1929. They were the underdogs playing against a team of big tough guys called the House of David. The Fredrickson Brothers Baseball Team beat them on a hot summer afternoon and celebrated their victory on the long journey home.

After that summer, Grandpa Herman and Fred, Martin, Axel, William, Nels, Joe, Edwin, Otto, Soren, Walter and Art didn't play ball together anymore, but they always remained best friends. They all lived close by the farm where they grew up. And they always loved baseball.

As their children grew up, they learned to play baseball, too. And those children are teaching their children to love baseball. They say around here that little Fredricksons are born with baseball gloves on their hands.

B ut chances are, none of them will play with so many brothers on one team. Grandpa Herman and Fred, Martin, Axel, William, Nels, Joe, Edwin, Otto, Soren, Walter and Art were one of a kind.

# Author's Note

The Fredrickson Brothers Baseball team was formed in Eidswold, Minnesota (near present-day Lakeville), in 1927. The family also included two brothers who did not survive to adulthood — an infant and Jens, who died at age 14. The brothers played traveling amateur ball until 1929. Their parents, Nels and Emelia Fredrickson, never saw them play because their strict religious background forbade any unnecessary activity on Sunday. The family's love of baseball, however, was stronger than their opposition, and today the ranks of amateur teams throughout southern Minnesota are filled with the Fredrickson brothers' progeny. At a family reunion in 1981, more than 500 Fredricksons in attendance formed eight ball teams for a friendly tournament. The ball field in Elko, Minn., is called Fredrickson Field in honor of the family's past and present involvement in the sport.

Though the team disbanded after their victory at the 1929 county fair, the brothers never allowed the ties that bound them as family to weaken. None moved farther away than Northfield, 13 miles southeast of Eisdwold. Edwin, born in 1901, lived in a house on his parents' original property until his death in 1996. Arthur, the youngest brother, was the last surviving member of the team; he passed away July 10, 2001.

Herman Fredrickson was the author's father-in-law, aka "Grandpa Herman" to her four children — Emilia, Eric, Ellie and Kathryn — and "Dad" to her husband Duane. Herman and Eleanor Fredrickson married in 1932 and had six children: Eldora, Dale (Skip), Myrna, Phyllis, Bob and Duane. Herman established his business, Fredrickson Lumber and Construction, on his father's property in 1958. The business is currently owned by Herman's son Skip.

The Fredrickson Brothers are honored in a display at The National Baseball Hall of Fame & Museum in Cooperstown, N.Y. The Hall of Fame recognizes 22 all-brother baseball teams, dating from the 1860s. The Fredricksons and one other family (the Acerras from Long Branch, N.J.) hold the record for the most brothers with 12 on one team. More information about the family team can be found at The National Baseball Hall of Fame & Museum Research Library or the Minnesota Historical Society.

## About the Author

Anne Fredrickson was raised in La Crosse, Wis., where she learned to play baseball with her two brothers. She earned a degree in journalism from the University of St. Thomas in St. Paul, Minn., and is a freelance writer and editor. She lives on a hobby farm in Northfield, Minn., with her husband Duane and four children. Her home is a portion of the farm formerly owned by Otto Fredrickson, the organizer of the Fredrickson Brothers team. Though her parents raised her to the sounds of Bob Uecker and the Milwaukee Brewers, she has converted to a Minnesota Twins fan. And despite the talent in her in-laws' family, she throws like a girl.

Anne Fredrickson can be contacted at whitebarnbooks.com.

## About the Illustrator

Kathryn Weaver lives in Overland Park, Kansas, and attends St. Olaf College (Class of 2011) in Northfield, Minnesota. Her favorite hobbies include reading, writing, drawing and playing clarinet. Though she loves nineteenth-century literature, art and costume design, she hopes to become a medical illustrator. She enjoys waterskiing and wakeboarding, but despite numerous attempts, she has never taken to any other sports — even baseball.